William Carey Richards

The Mountain Anthem

The Beatitudes in Rhythmic Echoes

William Carey Richards

The Mountain Anthem
The Beatitudes in Rhythmic Echoes

ISBN/EAN: 9783337289690

Printed in Europe, USA, Canada, Australia, Japan

Cover: Foto ©Thomas Meinert / pixelio.de

More available books at **www.hansebooks.com**

The
BEATITUDES
in rhythmic
Echoes.

THE

MOUNTAIN ANTHEM

The Beatitudes in Rhythmic Echoes

BY

WILLIAM C. RICHARDS

AUTHOR OF "THE LORD IS MY SHEPHERD," — THE TWENTY-THIRD
PSALM IN SONG AND SONNET

———————

BOSTON
LEE AND SHEPARD, PUBLISHERS
NEW YORK
CHARLES T. DILLINGHAM
1885

THE BEATITUDES.

1. And seeing the multitudes, he went up into a mountain; and when he was set, his disciples came unto him:

2. And he opened his mouth, and taught them, saying,

3. Blessed are the poor in spirit: for theirs is the kingdom of heaven.

4. Blessed are they that mourn: for they shall be comforted.

5. Blessed are the meek: for they shall inherit the earth.

6. Blessed are they which do hunger and thirst after righteousness: for they shall be filled.

7. Blessed are the merciful: for they shall obtain mercy.

8. Blessed are the pure in heart: for they shall see God.

9. Blessed are the peacemakers: for they shall be called the children of God.

10. Blessed are they which are persecuted for righteousness' sake: for theirs is the kingdom of heaven.

11. Blessed are ye, when men shall revile you, and persecute you, and shall say all manner of evil against you falsely, for my sake.

12. Rejoice, and be exceeding glad: for great is your reward in heaven: for so persecuted they the prophets which were before you.

Who of human birth are blessèd,
　　While to sorrow born, and sin?
Have earth's mightiest kings professèd
　　Bliss from crown and throne to win?
Of the richest or the strongest,
　　Of the wisest of their day,
Of those grasping gains the longest,
　　Dare we "They are blessèd" say?

"No," they answer through the ages, —
　　The illustrious ones of old,
Rulers, warriors, bards, and sages, —
　　Famed for pomp or power or gold.
Solomon his matchless glory
　　Counted vanity at best:
Where before or since, in story,
　　Shall we urge the empty quest?

He, of truth the perfect teacher, —
  Son of man, and God's own Son,
Seaside priest and hillside preacher, —
  Has the marvellous problem done.
From His mountain pulpit olden,
  Dropped the sweet Beatitudes,
Echoing here, their precepts golden
  Chime with rhythmic interludes.

8

THE POOR IN SPIRIT.

" Blessed are the poor in spirit : for theirs is the kingdom of Heaven."

Oh, blessed poor, who more than earth
    Shall at earth's close inherit !
Not squalid state, or abject birth,
    Infolds this priceless merit.
Not weary wanderers of the street,
With haggard eyes and halting feet,
This heirship's strange conditions meet :
    It reads, " The poor in spirit."

Yet earthly rank, or low or high,
    Sets to this class no limit,
Not boundless wealth can glorify —
    Nor poverty can dim it ;
It is the temper of the soul,
Strength in Humility's control,
A life grace-moulded to its whole —
    For angels to esteem it.

9

Theirs is a kingdom evermore,
  Of such transcendent glory,
Its rank and royalty before —
  Fade the proud realms of story.
That, infinite in time and space ;
These, crowding each for narrow place :
That, ever young, though ages cease ;
  And these, how transitory !

Kingdom of heaven ; Kingdom of God,
  Ineffable possession
Of those who lowly paths have trod
  In life's unsummed procession, —
The poor in spirit, dead to pride,
Who worthless hold worth unallied
With merit of the Crucified,
  In life's and death's confession !

THE JOY OF SORROW.

" Blessed are they that mourn: for they shall be comforted."

LET me sing the joy of sorrow,
  And the blessedness of tears :
Not that they will cease to-morrow,
  When the storm-cloud disappears ;
But the sweetness still of weeping
  Daily tears o'er daily wrong,
And the happy gain of keeping
  Grief the burden of our song.

He who wept for woes of others,
  And who, sinless, grieved for sin,
Owns us, by our tears, as brothers,
  When our godly griefs begin.
They who mourn for their transgressions
  By His voice are comforted,
And in penitent confessions
  Drops of grateful joy they shed.

Misery alone in mourning,

Save for Christ, our eyes had known ;
Prodigals to God returning,

We make music in our moan :
Every tear of grief is gladness ;

Every sob its solace brings :
So, for sweetness in his sadness,

Still the mourner weeps and sings.

14

THE DOWER OF THE MEEK.

" Blessed are the meek: for they shall inherit the earth."

NOT for the spiritless, not for the craven,
  Not for the halting and of little worth,
Is the divine beatitude engraven, —
    "They shall possess the earth."

Yet for the meek the Master's Will devises
  (All unconditioned by caprice or chance,
Howe'er man's wit and wisdom it surprises)
    This vast inheritance.

The meek are blessed, for "they shall inherit"
  (So reads the immortal testament) "the earth;"
But unbelief denies the Will the merit
    Of operative worth.

17

The earth, it boasts, is heired by Alexanders,
  Who win and sway it by the crimsoned sword ;
It asks, with scorn, the names of meek commanders
  Time's chronicles afford.

Ah! not as spoils of war and captive's cession,
  And not its soil or sea, its gems and gold, —
Not thus the meek acquire, in real possession,
  The earth, to have and hold.

There is a tenure larger and unwasting —
  The hold of Cæsars is, at best, but brief :
All mortal fiefs to mortal ends are hasting,
  And leave but loss and grief.

The meek of earth are, like their Master, humble,
  And covet not the diadems they wear :
So, when the glittering baubles fade or crumble,
  Their treasures are not there.

Herein, their heritage of earth is vital —
· Than what they have of it, no more they would ;
For all their lack, they find divine requital,
    And even ill count good.

The earth is theirs because it is their Master's,
  In Him their heirship is of first descent ;
Alien awhile by sin and death's disasters,
    It will revert unspent.

And by and by, in God's Palingenēsis,
  All claims but theirs, and claimants, set aside,
With the "new earth," in never-ending leases,
    They shall be satisfied.

SPIRITUAL LONGINGS.

" Blessed are they which do hunger and thirst after righteousness : for they shall be filled."

With hunger wasted, and with thirst opprest,
How say we that the sons of earth are blest?
Blessed indeed, the hand that soothes their woe,
And the quick tears that for their suffering flow :
Hunger to feed, and thirst to satisfy,
Proud gifts of gold in blessedness outvie.

Hunger is pain, and thirst consuming fire ;
We covet not one hour the hot desire ;
No blessedness can crown the feverish state,
But murmurs only on our yearnings wait.
If bread and wine the famished one have filled,
The cry of hunger and of thirst is stilled.

There is a hunger and a thirst divine,
·For living bread and soul-reviving wine,
And in themselves a heavenly charm we own,
That kindles joy from fervent want alone.
They know how strong desire their souls can bless,
Who hunger feel, and thirst, for righteousness.

And hungering yet, though with sweet manna fed,
And thirsting yet, while to full fountains led,
The Master's parable unveiled they read ;
And ever on His righteousness to feed,
With hunger more, and thirst the deeper, willed,
They evermore with righteousness are filled.

25

THE MERCIFUL.

" Blessed are the merciful: for they shall obtain mercy."

How sweet among the words divine,
Which in the Mountain Sermon shine,
   Our anger and our hate to lull,
Or read or heard, by old or young,
Or in the tuneful anthem sung,
   Seem " Blessed are the merciful " !

As dew on withered bloom distils,
As Sleep with peace the vision fills
   Of eyes that for the morning wait —
Drops on the soul, with pity stirred,
The sooth of this sufficing word
   Of Jesus the compassionate :

'They who are merciful shall know
The grace of mercy in their woe,
    And freely reap what they have sown :'
Christ, in the world's forlornest hour,
Of pity the consummate flower,
    This gospel of His love made known.

Mercy that lifts the fallen up,
That presses to parched lips the cup,
    That softens wrath, and checks the rod,
That feels and weeps with hearts that break,
And does all this for Christ's sweet sake
    Shall find the mercy of our God.

Among the promises of grace,
That bloom throughout sin's desert place,
    What flower diviner may we cull,
Than this, — that, in the sure reward
Of mercy from their sovereign Lord,
    Thrice "blessed are the merciful"?

THE PURE IN HEART.

"Blessed are the pure in heart: for they shall see God."

O VISION of wonder!
When bursting asunder
The thick-folding clouds,
The veils and the shrouds,
That have hidden God's face from their eyes —
These melt like the mist
Which the sunbeams have kissed,
And the heavens wide parted,
Before the pure-hearted,
Reveal the All Holy and Wise!

Ah! who may behold Him
While splendors infold Him
That blind mortal sight —
As the sun hides the night, —
The splendors of pure righteousness?

Not doers of ill,

Blind slaves of their will ;

Not lovers of pleasure

In earth's mood and measure,

Not these God's beholding can bless.

The omniscient Teacher,

The Heaven-sent Preacher,

The shroud rends away

Of sin and of clay ;

And, as flowers break forth from the sod

By His cross and grace,

From Sin's desert place

From Fear's gloomy prison,

Pure souls are uprisen

And blessed, "for they shall see God."

THE PEACEMAKERS.

" Blessed are the peacemakers: for they shall be called the children of God."

" THE children of God ! "   Not a title of earth
    With this may be mated for glory ;
Into baseness it dwindles man's royalest birth,
    And shrouds all the great names of story.

" The children of God ! "   On whom of earth's sons
    Sheds this rank its ineffable lustre ?
What clime and what age shall reveal us the ones
    On whose foreheads such proud honors cluster ?

Not the lofty of state, nor the mighty of sword,
    Who with blood redden earth to its borders ;
Not they who with lustful ambitions are stirred,
    And drift on the tide of disorders :

Not of such are the children of God who are crowned
· In the sermon of Christ's benedictions :
Of lowlier stations and names they are found,
    And fewer by mournful restrictions.

Who, then, are these heroes, scarce known to earth's
        fame,
    Who with sonship to God are invested ?
On humble peacemakers, in spirit and name,
    This rank from the Prince of peace rested.

Oh ! blessed for earth and for heaven are they
    Who pour upon strife's angry billows
The oil of God's peace, their wrath to allay,
    That songs may break forth by their willows.

The children of God, through the peace of His Son,
    Of His kingdom of peace made partakers, —
When the turmoils and tumults of sin are all done,
    Thrice blessed shall be the peacemakers.

37

THE MARTYRS OF RIGHTEOUSNESS.

" Blessed are they which are persecuted for righteousness' sake : for theirs is the kingdom of heaven."

OUT of the dungeon and the flame,
 Lo! strains of rapture break ;
And whispers sweet of Jesus' name
 Hallow the martyr's stake.
Apostles, saints, and humble men,
 Mothers, and maidens young,
From gibbet, rack, and lion's den,
 That precious name have sung.

And these are blessed in their stress
 Of torture and of death,
Who paid the price of righteousness
 With ebbing blood and breath ;

For, on the Mount the Master said,
　　Of sufferers for His sake, —
" Earth's crowns denied to them, instead
　　My kingdom they shall take."

The fiery stake and headsman's sword
　　To-day their lust forbear ;
Soul-freedom, — that immortal word —
　　Rings through and through the air :
Yet echoing from the sacred hill,
　　In all its force renewed,
We hear, with faith and gladness still,
　　This old beatitude.

For foes within and foes without
　　Raise crosses for us yet :
Within, fierce passions, pride, and doubt
　　Our wayward wills beset ;
Without, are mockers of our faith,
　　And sharp as swords their hate,
So, still on what the Master saith
　　In humble trust we wait.

Hate's fires may kindle to new heat,
  Her racks their pangs renew,
While good and ill in conflict meet,
  Till all things are made new.
If so, though I should feel the flame,
  Or tyrant's wrath endure,
'Twere bliss to hear my Lord exclaim,
  "Thy martyr-crown is sure!"